Explore THE Library

BOOK A/B

by
Jeri S. Cipriano

Scholastic Inc.

For Rachel,
who never stops
wondering
why

Thank you to Susan Frey, librarian, Springhurdst Elementary School, Dobbs Ferry, New York, for her time and cooperation.

Senior Vice President, Director of Education: Dr. Ernest Fleishman
Editor in Chief: Catherine Vanderhoof
Managing Editor: Sandy Kelley
Vice President, Director, Editorial Design and Production: Will Kefauver
Art Director: Joan Michael
Designer: Peg Reyes
Cover: Kevin O'Malley
Illustrators: Teresa Anderko, Rita Lascaro
Assistant Production Director: Bryan Samolinski

1 2 3 4 5 6 7 8 9 10 **14** 99 98 97 96 95

Table of Contents

Books of wonder, books of fun,
Books to read when day is done.
Books of tales and books of fact,
Books to teach you this and that.

Books of people and books that tell
Of magic tales where all ends well.
Books so silly and books so true,
Hundreds of books are waiting for you.

Introduction

A book can take you any place you want to go. Travel back in time. Rocket into the future. Meet famous people.

The library is filled with books. It has magazines, tapes, and videos, too. You can learn how to use the library. This book will help you. So get set for a big adventure!

Library Rules

Years ago, some libraries had sinks. Children had to wash their hands before they could touch a book!

What are your library's rules? Write them below.

Write on the Mark!

What if you are reading a book and have to stop for a while? You don't want to lose your place. Leaving a book open could break its cover. Folding down a corner of a page will make the pages weak.

bookmark. You'll find one just for you inside the back cover.

Cut out your bookmark. Write your name at the top. Then come up with a **motto,** or saying, that tells what you think about books

Cover to Cover

Most stories have three parts: a beginning, a middle, and an end. Books have different parts too. Each part tells something important.

Every book has a front cover, a back cover, and a spine. (The **spine** is the part you see when the book is on a shelf.) The name, or **title,** of the book is on the front cover. Sometimes you can tell what a book is about by reading its back cover.

"Gobble, gobble. What will the dragon eat next?"

THE HUNGRY DRAGON

THE HUNGRY DRAGON

Find the title *Explore the Library* on the cover of this book.

What other writing is on the cover?

_____

Tell about the art on the cover. What does it make you think of?

_____

Look at the back cover. Read what it says.
Write down two questions you think this book will answer.

_____

_____

_____

_____

Parts of a Book

When you read, you start at the beginning.
The first page of a book is called the **title page.**
What does it tell you?

THE HUNGRY DRAGON

By M.T. Plate
illustrated by Noah Ink

Lotta Books Company
New York

1. What is the **title,** or name, of this book?_____

2. Who is the **author,** or writer, of this book? _____

3. Who **illustrated,** or drew the pictures? _____

4. What company **published,** or printed, the book? _____

5. In what **city** is the publishing company found? _____

Look at the title page of *Explore the Library.*
You can tell that this book is part of a series of books.
Which book do you have? _____
Who wrote the book? _____

What company published the book? _____

Title and Copyright

Choose a book and open it to the title page.
Tell about your book on the lines below.

Title:_____

Author:_____

Illustrator:_____

Publisher: _____

Place of publication:_____

From the title, can you guess what the book will be about?
Write your guess: _____

_____

_____

Did you ever wonder when a book was first printed? Turn to page 2 to find out. The little ©, or **copyright,** tells the year the book was printed. Find the copyright page of your book. When was the book printed?

_____

Suppose you want to know what the newest computers can do. You find a book that was copyrighted 10 years ago. Would this book be useful to you? Why or why not?

_____

Check It Out!

Your school library has a special system for borrowing books. You may have to fill out a card that looks something like the one below. Fill it in for practice. Write the title and author of a favorite book. Write today's date, your name, and your room number or teacher's name.

	AUTHOR	
	TITLE	
DATE ` DUE	BORROWER'S NAME	ROOM NUMBER

Your Neighborhood Library

To borrow a book from a **public library,** you must have a **library card.** Getting a card is simple. Visit your neighborhood library and speak to the librarian. He or she will give you a card to fill out. (Sometimes a parent or guardian must sign the card too.) Then your library card will come in the mail! For practice, fill in the card below.

CENTRAL CITY PUBLIC LIBRARY

No._____

EXPIRES_____

===
DO NOT WRITE ABOVE THIS LINE

I promise to take good care of the books and other materials I use in the library and at home and to obey the rules of the library.

Name (print) _____

Home address_____

Apt. #_____   Zip _____ Phone _____

Name on mailbox _____

School _____Grade_____ Age _____

Where can you get a book about trees? At a branch library!

More Than Just Books

Libraries have more than just books.
Some even have animals for people to borrow!
Visit your school library. Check the kinds of
materials you find.

___ **books to borrow**

___ **computers**

___ **videos,
audiotapes, CDs**

___ **globes, maps**

___ **magazines
and newspapers**

___ **reference books**

Did you find anything else? Write it on the line.

_____

Suppose you need to answer the questions below. Where
would you look for the information? Find your answers
in the list above. The first one is done for you.

1. When was the light bulb invented? and by whom?
I would use a reference book _____ .

2. Where is the Pacific Ocean?
I would use _____

3. What happened in your favorite comic strip?
I would use _____ .

4. How does the song "This Little Planet" sound?
I would use _____ .

5. What is another book by your favorite author?
I would use _____ .

Read a Table of Contents

Suppose you are thinking of getting a pet. You look for a book about puppies. How can you tell if it has the kind of information you want?

Look at the **table of contents.**

It gives you the name of every chapter in the book. It also tells the page on which each chapter begins. Use this table of contents to answer the questions on the next page.

TABLE OF CONTENTS

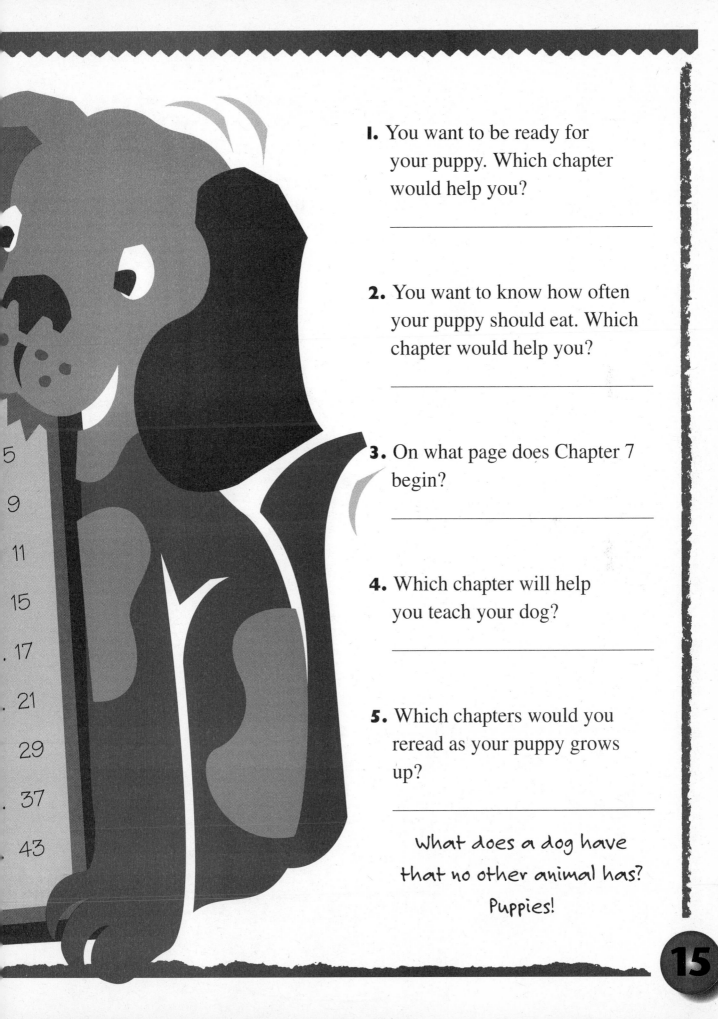

1. You want to be ready for your puppy. Which chapter would help you?

_____

2. You want to know how often your puppy should eat. Which chapter would help you?

_____

3. On what page does Chapter 7 begin?

_____

4. Which chapter will help you teach your dog?

_____

5. Which chapters would you reread as your puppy grows up?

_____

What does a dog have
that no other animal has?
Puppies!

Make a Table of Contents

Kreepers, the kitchen witch, wrote a book of recipes. Here are the chapter titles and the pages on which they begin. Help Kreepers complete the table of contents. Write the chapter titles and pages in order on the lines.

Table of Contents

Chapter Title

Page

Chapter 1: _____

Chapter 2: _____

Chapter 3: _____

Chapter 4: _____

Chapter 5: _____

Chapter 6: _____

Chapter 7: _____

Chapter 8: _____

Kreepers has a riddle for you. Here it is:

What makes a cookbook exciting?

Answer: It has many _____ chapters!

Give up? To get the answer, write the first letter of each chapter title you listed, in order.

Different Kinds of Books

Like people, no two books are exactly alike. **Fiction** books tell make-believe stories. **Nonfiction** books give facts about things in the real world. One kind of nonfiction book tells about the lives of famous people. These books are called **biographies.**

Look around your classroom or library. Find examples of each kind of book. Write the titles on the lines. Put checks next to your favorite books in each list.

Fiction	Nonfiction	Biographies
Fox Outfoxed	Snakes	The Wright Brothers

Ima Klutz tripped on the way to the library. These books fell out of her bookbag. What sort of books does Ima like? Write **F** for **fiction,** **NF** for **nonfiction,** or **B** for **biography** on each book.

Read an Index

At the back of some nonfiction books is an **index.** The index tells more than the table of contents. It lists most subjects covered in the book.

Subjects are listed in A-B-C order. Find the subject you need. Then turn to the page or pages listed next to the subject.

Here is part of the index from the puppy book.

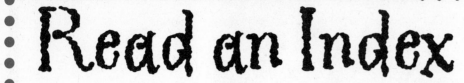

Index

Write the page(s) that would answer each question.

1. How often should you give your dog a bath? _____

2. What are some breeds of dogs? _____

3. What do you do when your dog has an "accident"? _____

4. How much exercise do dogs need? _____

5. How do you stop a dog from barking? _____

Visit your library. Find a book that has an index. Take the first letter of your name. Write some subjects that appear under that letter.

_____

_____

_____

_____

Pick one subject from your list. Turn to the pages listed in the index. Write something interesting you have learned.

_____

_____

_____

_____

How can you tell a dogwood tree? By its bark!

Make an Index

Juan Point wrote a book about board games. He made a list of all the games in his book and on what pages they are found. Help him put his index in A-B-C order. Look at the first letter of each word on the list.

Words that begin with the letter *a* should go first. If there are no *a* words, look for words that begin with *b*, and so on. If the first letters are the same, look at the second letters.

INDEX
Checkers, 5
Bingo, 9
Parcheesi, 10
Sorry, 11
Clue, 12-13
Scrabble, 14
Monopoly, 15-17

Write Juan's index in A-B-C order on the lines.

INDEX

Fact or Fiction?

A library is like a supermarket. Things are set up in a certain way. Once you know the setup, you will be able to find what you want.

Would you like a good story to read? Then go to the **fiction** section. You'll see that fiction books have letters only on their spines.

Want to know some facts about soccer? Then go to the **nonfiction** section. Nonfiction books have numbers <u>and</u> letters on their spines.

Which is which? Look at the book titles below. Write **F** for **fiction** under the books about make-believe things. Write **NF** for **nonfiction** under books that tell about real things.

Rey   CURIOUS GEORGE   R

Selsam   A First Look at SNAKES   597.96S

RYLANT   Henry and Mudge   R

MERCER   STATUE OF LIBERTY   974.71M

As Easy as A-B-C

Fiction books are put on shelves in alphabetical, or A-B-C, order. They are put in order by authors' **last names.** Sometimes authors have the same last names. When this happens, the books are then put in order by the authors' first names. For example, a book by Caroline Arnold would come before one by Eric Arnold.

What is this picture? Connect the words in alphabetical order to find out.

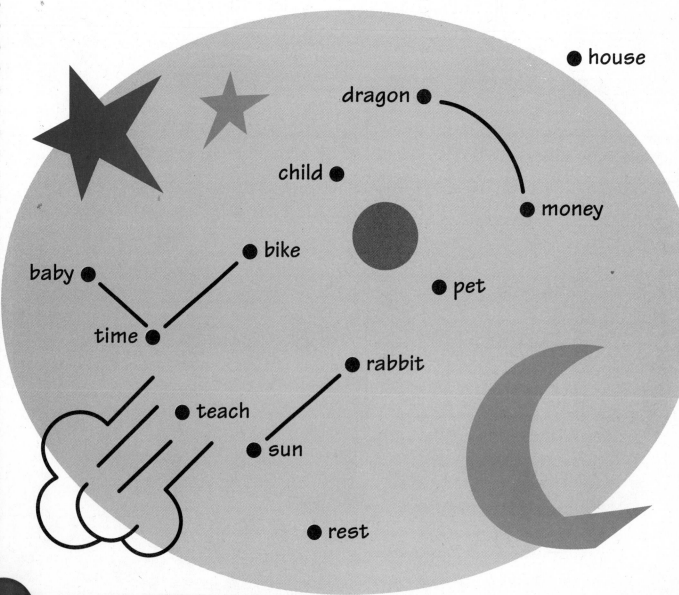

Minnie Pages wants to return these books to the library shelf. Please help her by putting them in the correct alphabetical order. Write the **last name** of each author, in order, on the lines.

Peggy Parish — AMELIA BEDELIA

David Adler — CAM JANSEN

Jane Yolen — OWL MOON

Arnold Lobel — FROG AND TOAD

James Marshall — FOX ON WHEELS

Maurice Sendak — PIERRE

William Steig — DOCTOR DE SOTO

1. ___ ___ ___ ___ (5)
2. ___ ___ ___ ___ ___
3. ___ ___ ___ (4) ___ ___ ___ ___
4. ___ ___ ___ (1) ___ ___
5. ___ ___ ___ (7) ___ ___
6. ___ (2) ___ (3) ___ ___
7. ___ ___ ___ (6) ___

Here's a riddle for you:
Why is a strawberry like a book?
Look at the letters inside the circles. Write them in the spaces that match their numbers. (The first one is done for you.) Now you have the answer. Do you get it?

Answer:
Because (I)(1) (2) (3) (4) (5) (6) (7)

Call Numbers

Nonfiction books have numbers <u>and</u> letters on their spines. These are **call numbers.** They help you find books. The numbers are part of a plan called the **Dewey Decimal System.** In 1876, a librarian named Melvil Dewey divided all nonfiction books into 10 main subject groups. He gave each group a set of numbers. All the books with the same numbers are put on the shelves together.

Books with numbers between 500 and 599 have to do with science. Visit the nonfiction section of your library. Find a book that belongs to this science group. Write its title, author, and call number below. Then tell what this book is about.

Science 500-599

Technology 600-699

Reference 000-099

Recreation 700-799

Title: _____

Author: _____

Call number: _____

This book is about: _____

_____

_____

_____

_____

Numbers, Please

Nonfiction books are put in order by their **numbers.** This is because their **subjects** are more important than their authors' names. You need to know <u>what</u> a book is about. Then you can decide if it has the right information for you.

Aliki	Simon	ALIKI	Parish	SELSAM
DINOSAUR BONES	The Smallest Dinosaurs	Wild and Woolly Mammoths	DINOSAUR TIME	Sea Monsters of Long Ago
567.9A	567.9S	569A	568P	568S

One book is out of order. Can you find it?
Write the name of the book that's in the wrong place.

Using a Card Catalog

The **catalog** is a file in A-B-C order of all the books in a library. You can look a book up by the subject you want to know about, the author who wrote it, or the title, if you know it. The card will tell you where in the library you can find the book you need.

Some school libraries have card files for their books. These files are kept in a set of drawers called a **card catalog.** Other libraries use computers.

Want a book on **holidays**? Then look in the drawer marked **H-J.** That drawer has cards that begin with the letters **H, I,** and **J.**

Which drawer would you look in for each of the following subjects?

ROBOTS _____   WHALES _____

COWBOYS _____   FRANCE _____

BASEBALL _____

Suppose you knew the title of a book, but not the author's name. How would you find it? You could look up the **title card** in the catalog.

Suppose you read a good book and wanted more by the same author. What would you do? You could look up the **author card** to find more books by that person.

Tell what kind of card you'd look for to find each thing below. Then tell which drawer you'd open. (Remember: You would look for an author's <u>last</u> name.) The first one is done for you.

	Type of Card	Drawer
Ramona the Brave	title	P-R
China		
Pancakes, Pancakes		
Eve Bunting		
Fairy tales		
Nate the Great		
Eric Carle		

Computers: At Your Fingertips

Many libraries have their catalog files on computers. The computer will help you find the book you want. This is called your <u>search</u>.

For most computer programs, you press a key that says **View catalog.** Then you have a choice. You can search for a **title,** an **author,** or a **subject.**

Say you want the book *Dinosaurs That Swam and Flew.* You would choose **title.** Then you would type in the words of the title. Look at the next page to see what would come up on the computer screen.

size, pages, illustrated

Title: Dinosaurs That Swam and Flew by David C. Knight; illustrated by Lee J. Ames.
Author: Knight, David C.
Publisher: Englewood Cliffs, NJ: Prentice Hall, © 1984.
Collation: 64 p.: ill.: 24 cm.
Subject: Dinosaurs
Subject: Animal, Fossil
Location: IRV JUV: 567.9K (J Book)

could be found under these subjects too

children's book

Look at the last line. It says **Location.** This tells you how to find, or **locate,** your book. This book can be found in the children's section of the Irvington Library. The letters **JUV** stand for **juvenile,** which means "for children." The call number 567.9K would tell you where on the shelves to look.

Will Reed has a list of things to look for. Look at each item. For each, tell whether to make a **title, author,** or **subject** search. Then write the words that Will should enter into the computer. (The first one is done for you.)

	Kind of Search	Enter
1. The book *Chicken Jokes*	title	Chicken Jokes
2. Books by James Howe		
3. Books about dolphins		
4. The book *Strega Nona*		
5. Books about penguins		
6. Books by Beverly Cleary		
7. Books about frogs		
8. The book *Arthur's Valentine*		

What subject do snakes like? <u>Hiss</u>-tory!

Books About People

Books about the lives of famous people are called **biographies.** All biographies are grouped together in the library. They are arranged alphabetically by the <u>last name of the person written about</u> — not the author.

The biography *True Stories About Abraham Lincoln* is by Ruth Belov Gross. But it has the letter **L** on its spine, not *G*. The **L** stands for **Lincoln.**

Here are two biographies. Write the letter that would be on the spine of each book.

Helen Keller
by Margaret Davidson _____

The Story of George Washingtom Carver
by Eva Moore _____

Some libraries use the letter **B** to stand for **biography.** Others use the number **92**. What does your school library use?

_____

Library Hall of Fame

Choose a favorite book from your school library. Draw a picture to show what the book is about. Then fill in the lines on the next page. Be ready to tell why you think the book belongs in a "Library Hall of Fame."

The title of my book is

_____.

It was written by _____ and

illustrated by _____.

You can find it in the _____ section

of the library.

The book is about _____

_____

_____.

My picture shows _____

_____

_____

_____.

I think this book is great because _____

_____

_____

_____

Using References

Now you know how to use the library. You can find and borrow any book you like. Some books, however, never leave the library. They are called **reference** books. People read or <u>refer</u> to them when they want special information.

Here are three reference books you may know.

Dictionary:
a book that gives the meanings of words

Tell which reference book (dictionary, encyclopedia, or atlas) you would use to answer each question. Then pick a partner. Together, see how fast you can track down the answers. (Hint: Dictionaries and encyclopedias are in alphabetical order.)

1. Could you have a **zither** instead of buttons on a coat?

_____

_____

2. When was **television** invented?

_____

3. Is **Brazil** in South America or Africa?

_____

_____

Encyclopedia:
a set of books that have facts on many subjects

Atlas:
a book of maps

4. What does **chuckle** mean?

_____

_____

5. Is **Texas** north or south of Oklahoma?

_____

6. How many strings does a **guitar** have?

_____

_____

7. Would you use a **scone** in your hair?

_____

_____

8. Is **tail** or **tale** another word for <u>story</u>?

_____

When does Friday come
before Thursday?
In the dictionary!

What's the Story?

On page 46 is a reading log. Use it to keep track of the books you read. Here are some fun ideas to share.

The More the Merrier

Read a story with a partner. Talk about what happened in the story. Then work together. Make puppets or act out the story. You can dress as the characters. Can your classmates guess your book?

Who Am I?

Read a biography about a famous person from history. Dress as the person. Tell some facts about the person. See if your classmates can guess who you are.

Think of other famous people. Form a library search team. Find facts about these people from books or encyclopedias.

Show and Tell

Give a book talk about a favorite book. Tell whether the book is real (nonfiction) or make-believe (fiction). Mention the main characters. Tell something about the setting — where the story takes place. Add any other interesting details. But don't give away the ending!

Finding Facts

A **report** is different from a story. In a report, you tell true facts about your subject. You can give a report in person. Or you can write a report.

Here is part of a report on great horned owls:

Great horned owls lay their eggs in winter! The female lays two or three eggs. She looks for empty nests built by hawks, crows, or squirrels. If she can't find a ready-made nest, she will use a hole in a tree.

Both parents keep the eggs warm all through the winter. By spring, the young owls are already three months old. They are ready to leave the nest. Spring is when most baby birds and small animals are born. Yum! That's dinner for a strong young owl.

Owls are not like many other birds.
Write two facts that prove this statement true.

_____

_____

_____

_____

Just the Facts, Please

There are many ways to do **research,** or get information. One way is to talk to someone who knows the subject. Another way is to take out books about your topic.

Rachel wants to know more about guinea pigs. She finds a book in the library. Then she speaks with a pet-shop owner. First, she thinks of the questions she'd like to answer.

What are guinea pigs?

What do guinea pigs eat?

How do guinea pigs look?

Where do guinea pigs live?

Why do guinea pigs make good pets?

Here are some facts about guinea pigs. Which questions and answers go together? Draw a line to show a match.

Guinea pigs have four toes on their front feet. They have three toes on their back feet! They don't have any tail at all.

Guinea pigs are **not** pigs! They are rodents, like rats and mice. Rodents have two front teeth. (A guinea pig's teeth never stop growing!)

Guinea pigs eat vegetables and fruits such as lettuce, carrots, apples, pears.

Guinea pigs are gentle. They are easy to care for. They live in cages, but like to come out to play.

Guinea pigs live in warm places in South America. In the wild, they sleep in the day and come out at night.

Be an Expert!

Pretend there is an animal fair in your school. Get ready to be an animal expert. Follow each step.

Choose an animal you want to know more about.

_____

Write five or more questions you want to answer.

QUESTION 1:

_____

QUESTION 2:

_____

QUESTION 3:

_____

QUESTION 4:

_____

QUESTION 5:

_____

Now get ready to do a report. Draw or paste a picture of your animal in the box. Use the lines to write some facts for your report.

NAME OF ANIMAL:

_____

Library Hunt

You need to play this game in the library. Play alone or take turns with a friend. Have fun — and happy hunting!

What states share borders with Kansas?

_____

_____

What two countries border the United States?

_____

_____

Write the title of a book by James Howe.

_____

Write the names of two books that have to do with sharks.

_____

_____

When did Martin Luther King, Jr., die?

_____

Write the titles of two books by Marjorie Sharmat.

Who wrote the book *Princess Furball?*

_____

_____

Draw what a cornucopia
looks like.

Is the book *Strega Nona*
illustrated by Tomie dePaola?

_____

Could you learn about the customs
of Japan in the encyclopedia? Would
you look in Volume C or J? _____

Write two facts about a sloth.

_____

_____

Would a book with
a call number 591.4 be
fiction or nonfiction?
_____

**Does the copyright
appear on the title page?**
_____

Find a book about whales.
Write two facts.

_____

_____

_____

Find a biography.
Write its title here:

_____

_____

_____

45

Reading Log

Use this page to keep a record of your reading.

Title of Book and Author	Fiction or Nonfiction?	Rating (circle one)
		1 2 3
		1 2 3
		1 2 3
		1 2 3
		1 2 3
		1 2 3
		1 2 3
		1 2 3
		1 2 3
		1 2 3
		1 2 3
		1 2 3
		1 2 3

**mething cool
earned or liked:**

**Some words
I want to remember:**

Show What You Know!

What does the library have that makes it the tallest building?

To get the answer to the riddle, complete each sentence below. Write your answers in the puzzle. (The answers are all in this book.) The colored letters will spell the answer to the riddle.

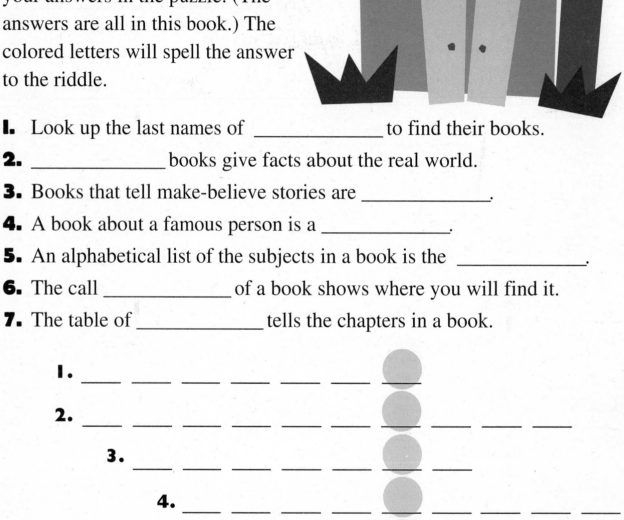

1. Look up the last names of _____ to find their books.

2. _____ books give facts about the real world.

3. Books that tell make-believe stories are _____.

4. A book about a famous person is a _____.

5. An alphabetical list of the subjects in a book is the _____.

6. The call _____ of a book shows where you will find it.

7. The table of _____ tells the chapters in a book.

1. ___ ___ ___ ___ ___ ___ ___

2. ___ ___ ___ ___ ___ ___ ___ ___ ___ ___

3. ___ ___ ___ ___ ___ ___

4. ___ ___ ___ ___ ___ ___ ___ ___

5. ___ ___ ___ ___ ___

6. ___ ___ ___ ___ ___

7. ___ ___ ___ ___ ___ ___ ___